S0-CAZ-103

FROGS

A PORTRAIT OF THE ANIMAL WORLD

ANDREW CLEAVE

TODTRI

Copyright © 1999 by Todtri Productions Limited.
All rights reserved. No part of this publication may be reproduced,
stored in a retrieval system or transmitted in any form by
any means electronic, mechanical, photocopying or otherwise,
without first obtaining written permission of the copyright owner.

This book was designed and produced by
TODTRI Book Publishers
P.O. Box 572, New York, NY 10116-0572
FAX: (212) 695-6984
e-mail: info@todtri.com

Printed and bound in Singapore

ISBN 1-57717-132-2

Author: Andrew Cleave

Publisher: Robert M. Tod
Senior Editor: Edward Douglas
Photo Editor: Linda Waldman
Book Designer: Mark Weinberg
Typesetting: Command-O Design

PHOTO CREDITS
Photo Source/Page Number

Peter Arnold, Inc.
Arnold Newman 67 (top)

James H. Carmichael, Jr. 3, 5, 6, 8–9, 10 (top), 11 (top & bottom),
14 (top), 15, 16, 17, 18 (top & bottom), 19, 20, 21, 22, 23,
26 (top & bottom), 27, 29, 30, 31, 33, 34 (top & bottom), 35, 36,
39 (top), 42 (top & bottom), 43 (top & bottom), 44–45, 46, 47,
48, 49, 50, 52, 53, 54 (top & bottom), 55, 56–57, 58, 59 (top),
61, 62, 63 (top & bottom), 64 (top & bottom), 66, 68, 69, 70, 71

David Liebman 38, 40–41

Joe McDonald 10 (bottom), 12, 24–25, 32, 37, 59 (bottom), 65

Photo Researchers, Inc.
Stephen Dalton 7, 13, 28
Tom McHugh 4
Karl H. Switak 60

Picture Perfect
Gerald Cubitt 51
Warren Jacobi 14 (bottom)
Stephen Kirkland 67

Roger Rageot/David Liebman 39 (botttom)

INTRODUCTION

The small pool trapped inside the flower of a bromeliad in a Costa Rican forest provides just enough water for this minute cross–banded tree frog, Smilisca phaeota. *In the rainy conditions of these forests, countless numbers of these tiny pools occur in the tree canopy, and the frogs need never come to the ground to find water for spawning.*

*C*atching tadpoles in a pond and taking them home to watch their development from wriggling black spheres with tails attached into miniature frogs or toads must have been a common introduction to natural history for many biologists. Evolution is compressed into just a few weeks as the tiny black egg, protected inside the clear jelly of the spawn, turns into a primitive fish-like creature barely capable of movement, then progresses through a series of changes of form and habits, until it becomes a tiny frog and leaves its watery habitat for a completely different environment on land.

There are very few habitats where frogs and toads can not be found. Apart from the sea, and the frozen polar regions, they have managed to exploit almost every type of aquatic and terrestrial habitat from lakes, ponds, swamps, and marshes to farmland, forests, and mountain slopes. Even deserts, some of the most inhospitable places on earth, have a few species living in them. Frogs and toads are even familiar to city dwellers, as some species are quite happy to live in garden ponds. Since ancient times, frogs have figured in art and literature, myths, and legends. Being such familiar creatures, and so numerous and widespread in the past, they have become a part of folklore in many parts of the world.

Despite all this familiarity, there is still much to learn about frogs and toads. New species are being discovered in tropical forests, more is being learned about the importance of frogs and toads in ecosystems, and worrying facts are emerging about the imminent extinction of certain species as their habitats are being destroyed.

Some species are very rare, restricted to a few localized areas, and there are extinctions from time to time as small populations suffer from some crisis in their habitat. However, there are many species that are widespread and abundant and are of great importance in their environment. They are important consumers of invertebrates, many of which are considered to be pest species, and they are themselves food for other higher organisms, forming an important link in the food chains in many habitats.

Everyone can recognize a frog or a toad and recount the basic details of their life story, but many people don't know the true range of species found around the world and the extraordinary adaptations they show in order to survive in different habitats.

The African bullfrog, Pyxicephalus adspersus, *like other large frogs, is not an active hunter. Rather than move about to seek out its food, it prefers to sit quietly and wait for a likely prey animal to appraoch. When the unwary victim is within striking distance, the bullfrog will attack and swallow its prey in one gulp. Bullfrogs feed on rodents, young waterfowl, small turtles, and even young frogs of their own kind.*

The barking tree frog, Hyla gratiosa, *occurs in the southeastern United States and earned its name from its persistent barking call, usually uttered from high up in a tree. As well as being a good climber, it can also burrow into damp soil. This is one of the most abundant tree frog species.*

CHARACTERISTICS OF FROGS AND TOADS

Frogs and toads are both amphibians belonging to the order Anura, which means that they have no tails. Other amphibians are the newts, salamanders, and axolotls, which all bear some form of tail and have similar life histories, developing from eggs into tadpoles, and then undergoing a metamorphosis into adults. All of the other amphibians have the ability to spend part of their lives in water and part as air breathers living on land.

Identifying Frogs and Toads

When scientists first began naming living things, very few species of frogs and toads were known. The common European frog, *Rana temporaria* became the frog, and the common European toad, *Bufo bufo*, became the toad. The frog has a smooth, slimy skin, and is a good jumper, while the toad has a dry warty skin and prefers to walk. As increasing numbers of new species were found, they were assigned names according to their body form; slimy species were "frogs," and warty species were "toads." As a general rule, toads laid their eggs in long strings of spawn, and frogs laid their eggs singly or in a mass of jelly. Today, all the tailless amphibians can be called frogs, with the family Bufondiae containing those species best known as toads—effectively, they are a subgroup within the larger family of frogs.

There are around 3,500 known species of frogs and toads distributed around the world. They all share very similar characteristics and are all recognizable as frogs or toads, but there are many differences between the species. Frogs and toads vary greatly in size, from the tiny glass frogs—often no more than 3/8 inch (1 cm) in length—up to the huge Goliath frog at over 12 inches (30 cm) long, and the bullfrogs of North America which reach 6 inches (15cm) in length.

Frogs and toads are among the most attractive of all vertebrates, with many of them having stunning coloration and patterns. The

FOLLOWING PAGE: The strawberry dart–poison frog, Dendrobates pumilio, from Costa Rica, is a small species that lives among the leaf litter on the forest floor, where it feeds on ants and other tiny invertebrates. Like the other poisonous species, it advertises its dangerous properties with striking colors.

Here a common frog, Rana temporaria, is seen leaping from a grassy bank into the water. Frogs of this species are noted for their extraordinary jumping abilities which enable them to make a rapid and effective escape from enemies.

The painted mantella frog, Mantella madagascariensis, uses its bold patterns and colors as a display. Like many small frogs, it is largely nocturnal in its habits, hiding from predators during daylight.

Hidden inside the stunning red lily from a Costa Rican rain forest is one of the smallest of all frogs, the diminutive small glass frog, Hylenidae. Small insects visiting the lily for its pollen are easy prey for this well–concealed frog.

The Colorado River toad, Bufo alvorius, is one of the largest species in the United States, and apart from its size, has no distinguishing markings, being mostly brownish–gray above and paler on the underside. Its skin produces poisonous secretions that predators find distasteful, so it is normally avoided.

tiny tree frogs of the tropical forests and the poisonous species of South America have dazzling colors which serve as warnings to predators. Others show beautiful shades of green and brown to help them blend with their surroundings. Frogs are also among the most vocal of vertebrates, most of them having the ability to produce some sounds. Much of the background noise in a tropical forest at night is produced by vocalizing frogs, with sounds ranging from high-pitched warbles to deep bass croaks. Often, whole populations will call in chorus, drowning out all the other calls of the night.

This sequence-shot of a common European frog, Rana temporaria, *jumping, demonstrates the amazing power and agility of these small creatures. What can't be shown here is the swiftness with which they spring into the air.*

The beautiful golden mantella frog, Mantella aurantiaca, from Madagascar is a very small species and one of the most colorful of all frogs. Despite its bright color, it is hard to find, because it is normally hidden in vegetation; however, it sometimes emerges in humid conditions.

The large African bullfrog, Pyxicephalus adspersus, is cryptically marked and difficult to observe, but its call is loud, far carrying, and especially impressive when combined in a chorus with the calls of other bullfrogs. Its huge mouth enables it to tackle large prey.

Frogs and toads are highly vocal creatures and produce a variety of distinctive sounds. In many species, such as in this male spadefoot toad, *Scaphiopus holbrooki*, from Florida, the calls are amplified by large vocal sacs, which are inflated during vocalization but reduced in size at other times.

Bright colors usually mean "I'm dangerous—leave me alone!" This tomato frog, *Dyscophus guineti*, from Madagascar, is adding to the warning by inflating its body to make it look even more threatening to a predator.

The Skin

The skin is a very important organ in frogs and toads. It is vital in maintaining water levels in their bodies and in facilitating the process of respiration. The two main layers of the skin, the epidermis on the outside, and the dermis on the inside, contain many specialized cells.

Mucus cells produce the slimy substance which helps keep the skin moist, and poison cells produce the toxins which many species release in order to defend themselves from predators. In the skin of toads the poison cells are grouped together in large enough clusters to form the characteristic warty glands on the surface of the skin.

The poison dart frogs of South America gained their name through the secretions of powerful poisons from their skins. These were captured by the native Indians living in the forests and used to poison the tips of

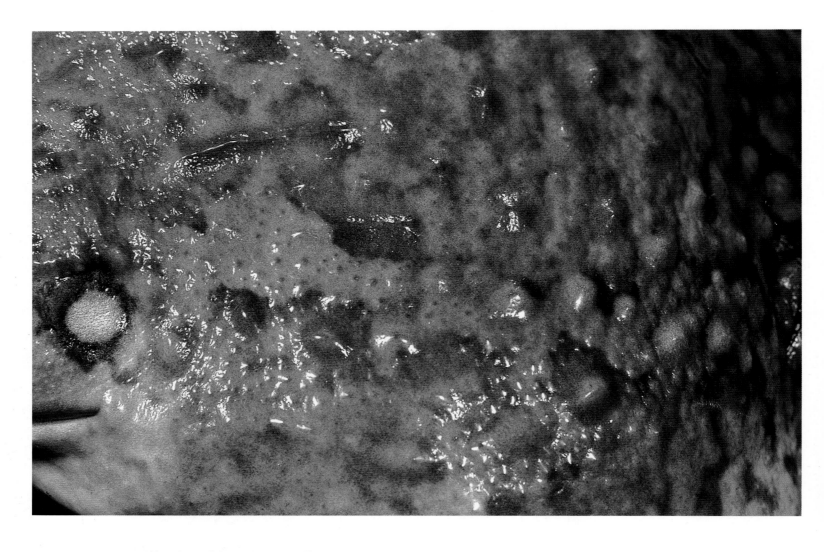

The skin of frogs is normally moist, and in many species contains glands which secrete a mucus to maintain the correct moisture level when the frog is out of water. The skin can be used for respiration, allowing the exchange of vital gases, and is also highly pigmented, aiding the frog's camouflage or mating displays. The skin of this African bullfrog, Pyxicephalus africanus, *is tough and protects it when it burrows to escape dry conditions.*

The dye–poison frog, Dendrobates tinctorius, *from the rain forests of Surinam has an unusual blue background color. This, plus its bold pattern of spots, is sufficiently startling to warn off predators. It is a small species that feeds mainly on ants and has a high number of poison glands in its skin.*

darts used for hunting. The poisons are so powerful, they can remain potent for up to a year on the tip of a dart. Captured frogs are usually held down with a stick, and the wooden tip of the dart, constructed with a groove along its length, is rubbed over the back of the frog. Enough poison is picked up to kill quite large prey.

Scattered among the other skin cells are pigmented cells known as chromatophores which give the skin its coloration and patterns. These cells can expand or contract and cause color changes in the skin, often in order to aid camouflage. Many species can modify their body color in order to suit their background, particularly the ground living species that rely on camouflage rather than poison for defense against predators.

The dart-poison frog, Epipedobates tricolor, from Ecuador is one of the species hunted in the forest by the indigenous tribes, who use the highly potent poison to tip darts for hunting.

The Amazon horned frog, Ceratophrys cornuta, inhabits the shady world of the forest floor where fallen leaves provide a mottled background. Its strange shape and swirling patterns break up its outline, making it far less conspicuous than more conventionally marked frogs.

Striking black and white markings leave predators in no doubt about the poisonous properties of this dart–poison frog, Dendrobates, from Surinam and northern Brazil.

The skin of the poisonous tree frog, Phrynohyas venulosa, exudes a secretion that is both highly sticky and irritating. A snake that comes in contact with this frog will find its jaw sealed shut by the substance on the frog's skin.

This dart–poison frog, Epipedobates tricolor, from Ecuador, has warning coloration which makes it very conspicuous. Despite its small size, it packs enough poison to make it dangerous to any predator.

*The brilliant
coloration on
the underside
of the Oriental
fire–bellied toad,*
Bufo orientalis,
*widespread
across north-
eastern Asia,
is used for
display during
courtship.
Its upperparts
have far less
conspicuous
green coloration.*

Respiration

Respiration is a vital process for all living organisms. It involves taking in oxygen and giving off carbon dioxide. Adult frogs and toads have small lungs which are ventilated by raising and lowering the floor of the mouth. This is easily observed by watching a frog at rest. Frogs can also breathe through their skins, as long as the surface is moist. Blood vessels run close to the surface of the skin, and a fine network of thin-walled capillaries spreads out to cover much of the surface area. About a quarter of the total oxygen requirement can be obtained in this way.

Some species, especially those that are almost completely aquatic, obtain most of their oxygen through the skin, and they often have special adaptations to help them. The skin may have many extra folds and look rather loose, or in the case of the so-called hairy frog, there may be many hair-like papillae growing out of the side of the body. These serve to increase the surface area of the body available for oxygen uptake. Terrestrial frogs generally prefer humid environments, in order to maintain the moisture levels of the skin and facilitate respiration.

Tadpoles have gills protruding from the side of the body at first, but as they develop, the gill becomes enclosed in a gill chamber on either side of the head. Tadpoles can also breathe through their skins, probably obtaining about half of their oxygen by this method. The surface area of a tadpole, relative to its body volume, is very large, due mainly to the presence of the long, thin tail; so gas exchange through the skin is a very important part of respiration.

Food and Diet
Adult frogs and toads are all carnivores, taking a wide variety of food items ranging from tiny insects to small birds, mammals, and reptiles. For almost all species, the food must be living, as they normally locate their prey by detecting movement. There is a limit to the size of prey that frogs and toads can consume, as all food must be swallowed whole. Frogs have no significant teeth, but they do have large gaping mouths, so they can gulp down their prey in one go. There are a few exceptions to this, as some species have occasionally been known to take carrion or ingest plant material, but for most species, live food is essential.

The Diet of Tadpoles
Tadpoles often have a more varied diet, taking plant material, microscopic organisms, and carrion where available. Tadpoles have simple, beak-like mouths surrounded by rows of rasping "teeth" that are used to scrape off microscopic algae from plant surfaces, pick up detritus from the bed of ponds, or scrape the surface layers from dead aquatic creatures. Much of the food obtained in this way is difficult to digest, and tadpoles have a long digestive tract which can sometimes be seen coiled inside the body.

A few species are filter feeders, taking minute particles from the water they are swimming in. They draw in a current of water and filter out suspended particles of organic matter; the water then passes on over the gills where oxygen is removed, before it leaves the body through the gill chambers. There are even a few cannibalistic species that eat frogs eggs or

The surface area of a tadpole, which includes the tail, is large enough to play an important part in respiration. About one–half of the tadpole's oxygen is obtained through its skin.

other small tadpoles. Some species eat only eggs of their own kind, while others, living in rich habitats where several species occur, may take the eggs and young of other species.

Hunting Techniques

The adults of most species are opportunistic feeders, taking whatever prey happens to present itself in an advantageous way. If they remain in a single habitat, such as a weed-filled pond, their prey is likely to be aquatic in nature, whereas if they live on a forest floor, they are more likely to take terrestrial insects. Many species remain concealed for much of the day, relying on their camouflage, or they partly bury themselves in soil or leaves. There is a risk that if they wander around actively seeking prey, they will end up as food themselves. If an unsuspecting prey species passes close enough to a concealed frog, it will be snapped up at once.

At night, nocturnal frogs and toads move around in their habitats seeking suitable food. They may wander randomly, taking whatever food they can catch, or they may congregate in likely places, such as near a street light, so that they can pick off night–flying insects, like moths, attracted by the brightness.

Some of the larger and less agile species, such as bullfrogs, use a "wait and see" strategy to find their food. They are capable of taking large, but wary and fast-moving prey, such as small rodents; so keeping still and quiet, and relying on camouflage, is a far better way of getting close to a mouse. They may take only one or two prey animals a day, but these will be large, nutrient rich meals which will sustain them for long periods.

FOLLOWING PAGE: The forward–looking eyes of the large African bullfrog enable it to focus directly on its prey, and its huge mouth means that it can ingest quite large organisms in one gulp.

Epiphytic brome-liads growing high up in a Costa Rican rainforest provide a safe hiding place for these tropical tree frogs and also act as miniature pools for them to moisten their skins in. The leaves capture ample water from the frequent tropical storms.

A beautiful or-chid in a Peruvian forest provides a good vantage point for a tiny tree frog, Hyla leucophyllata, *to perch on and wait for visiting insects.*

Long, flexible limbs, suction pads for feet, and a slender, athletic body are ideal for climbing through vegetation in pursuit of insect prey. Moreover, green coloration provides the perfect camouflage for the diminutive red–eyed tree frog.

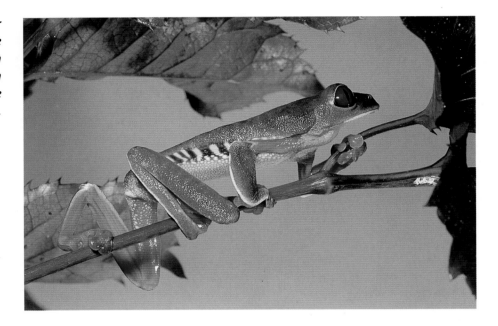

Large, protruding eyes, such as these on the golden–eyed tree frog, Phryonhyas venulosa, from Costa Rica, are typical of most frog species and are an adaptation to hunting in low light conditions. Frogs have good eyesight which enables them to detect the movement of their prey and approaching predators. They can also distinguish colors.

The smaller, lightweight species, such as the glass frogs and tree frogs have greater agility and rapid reactions, and can leap after a flying insect with considerable success. They will need to take quite a number of these, however, as tiny insects have less food value.

When prey is sighted, it is watched for a few seconds without any movement by the frog. It may then adjust its position slightly to get a better look, and in some species there may be some twitching of the toes and limbs. This is thought to have some effect on certain insects, possibly attracting them closer to the frog. If the prey stops moving, the frog is unlikely to do anything, but if it moves again it will prepare to strike. It will probably raise itself a little and push the body forward, and then prepare the tongue for the strike.

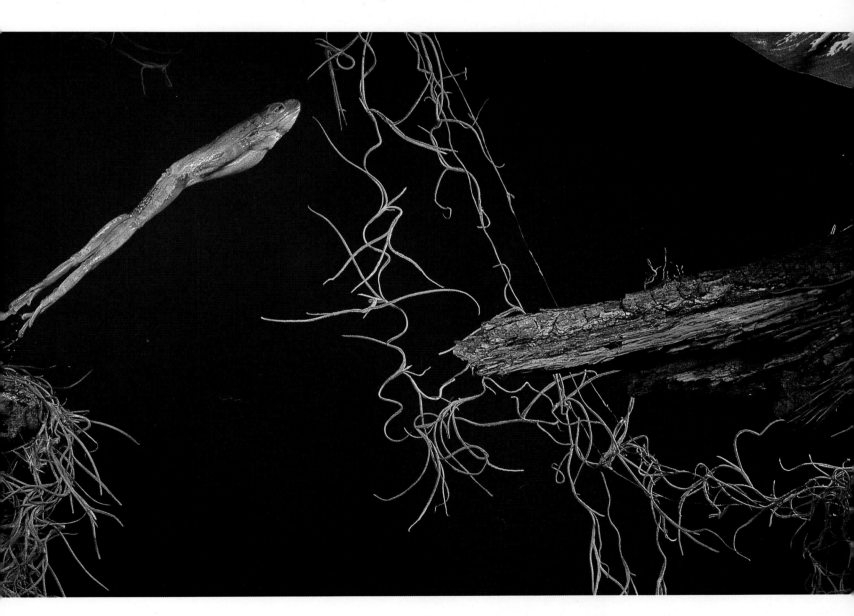

Although scrambling through the vegetation, and clinging to bark is the normal habit of the Cuban tree frog, it can jump easily from one tree to another if necessary. Its powerful hind legs propel it forwards, while the front legs remain at its side until ready to land.

The Tongue and Mouth

Most species have long sticky tongues which are hinged at the front of the mouth. This can be shot forward with great speed and accuracy to capture small prey species like earthworms or beetles. The mucus coating of the tongue is sufficiently sticky to hold the prey on the tongue while it is whipped back into the mouth for swallowing. This fly-paper tongue is a very useful adaptation to capturing small, fast-moving prey, and has enabled frogs and toads to exploit a food source that is difficult for other vertebrates to make use of. It is such

a rapid process that is also very difficult for the human eye to see much of the detail. It was not until high-speed photography was developed that this process was fully understood.

Not all species have sticky tongues of this type. The fire-bellied toads, for example, simply lunge forward and envelop the prey in their mouths. They may use their hands to help force the prey in and secure it before swallowing. Aquatic species, like the African clawed toad and the Surinam toad have no tongues. They depend on their hands to capture their food. Their normal feeding habit is

Since frogs and toads have no teeth, they must use their large mouths to swallow food whole. Here a common European toad, Bufo bufo, has just caught an earthworm with its long sticky tongue.

Horned frogs, such as this species from Surinam, are large, strong frogs with bulky bodies and short powerful limbs. The "horns" above the eyes help break up the outline of the body. All of the horned frogs have large powerful jaws and are capable of taking large prey.

to sit absolutely still in the water with their forearms and fingertips spread out in front of them. If they spot moving prey, they will seize it. However, even in very murky conditions, they can locate prey by a very sensitive sense of touch. As soon as prey is detected, it is forced towards the huge mouth with the hands while the body lunges forward to prevent escape. For instance, as large earthworms are manipulated into the best position for swallowing, the hands are used to hold the prey firmly.

Frogs have no recognizable teeth, but they do often have rows of notches on the jaws, or rough projections on the roof of the mouth, that help to grip prey during swallowing. Food is not chewed or broken up in any way; it has to be swallowed whole, and usually while it is still alive. Swallowing itself seems to be a rather strenuous process involving gulping and pressing the eyes down into their sockets—sometimes singly, sometimes together—in order to help force the food down into the esophagus. The interior of the mouth is well lubricated with mucus to aid swallowing. Tiny insects are no problem, but species which take large earthworms or small rodents have to work hard to get their food into their bodies.

The spiny-headed tree frog, Anotheca spinosa, *is indeed a curious and unusual creature. This rare species—a native of the Costa Rican rain forest—though a slight, dimuntive frog, is well adapted for self defense. The spines on its head discourage predators from making an attack.*

An earthworm is an easy meal for a horned frog, Ceratophrys ornata, *whose large mouth and strong jaws can cope with the full length of its wriggling prey. Frogs gulp their food and ingest it as quickly as possible and then retire to a safe place to digest the meal.*

BEGINNING THE LIFE CYCLE

Many of the well-known characteristics of frogs and toads, such as their calls, and their interesting markings, have evolved to help during courtship and mating. The life histories of the commoner species are well known and often taught to children in school. Many naturalists eagerly await the spring breeding season when frogs and toads converge on their breeding ponds and start their courtship behavior as a prelude to spawning. The frog and toad spawn is followed by swarms of wriggling black tadpoles, and then the migration of hundreds of tiny frogs and toads from the ponds back into the surrounding countryside.

This is a familiar story, and for many species this pattern of reproduction is followed with little variation. However, among the many hundreds of species there are variations on this theme. Fertilization may be external or internal; the spawn may be in clumps, strings, or single eggs; it may be laid in or out of water; the tadpoles may or may not feed; or there may be no tadpoles at all, the tiny froglets emerging directly from the eggs, or in some cases, being born live as miniature versions of the adults.

Breeding Season

Spring time is the traditional breeding season for most species in temperate climates. Many of them will have hibernated in the winter, and the onset of warmer weather will have stimulated them to become active. Weather conditions are suitable then as the water levels are usually high, invertebrate populations are

In temperate regions, spring is the start of the breeding sesaon due to warmer weather and the availabilty of a larger supply of invertebrates for food. There is no set breeding season in the tropics, but the arrival of rains encourages spawning in the many small pools of water that are created.

The American toad is a very widespread species across the eastern United States, inhabiting a range of habitats from gardens to mountain slopes. It requires shallow water for breeding, hiding places under logs or stones, and a variety of invertebrates for food.

Communication between frogs usually takes the form of calling or using bright colors and display behavior. Rivals, like these Costa Rican tree frogs, Hyla rosenbergi, may sometimes jostle for position on a favored leaf. Males guard nesting depressions they excavate in damp ground.

The rain forests of Costa Rica are home to a huge variety of tree frogs, a group that shows a great range of colors. Agalychnis callidryas, the red-eyed tree frog, uses its vivid flank markings in courtship displays.

increasing after the cold of the winter, and there is the prospect of warmer weather ahead to speed the development of the tadpoles.

In tropical climates there may be no definite breeding season, the frogs rely instead on rainy seasons to provide sufficient water in small pools to allow breeding. A few species, such as those living in very arid regions with an unreliable annual rainfall, may have to wait for more than a year for there to be enough water to stimulate breeding

Courtship

For the majority of species, the breeding season commences with a mass gathering at a favored breeding site. Often, these are well known, traditional sites, and the times of arrival at them can be predicted with reasonable accuracy. The stimulus to congregate at a pond is usually initiated by the onset of longer days and a rise in temperature. This causes certain hormonal changes in the bodies of the frogs that bring them into breeding condition. In the case of females, the ovaries begin egg production, while the testes of the males start to produce sperm.

Other changes occur at the same time, and these may be both physical and behavioral. Males of many species produce nuptial pads, special thickened structures on the hands that enable them to grip the slippery bodies of the females during mating. Males may also undergo some color changes linked to courtship. The normally subdued colors of the male European frog, for example, are brighter, and the light patch under the chin becomes blue-tinged and far more conspicuous when the head is held up out of the water. Females become fatter, but this is due to the increasing size of the ovaries as the eggs develop. At this stage the eggs do not have the full thickness of protective jelly around them.

Male frogs are usually smaller than females, although the size difference is not always as well pronounced as in these masked puddle frogs, Smilisca, *from Costa Rica. During mating the male clasps the female from above, holding onto her slippery body with thickened "nuptial pads" on the front feet.*

35

As this female Cuban tree frog releases eggs into the water, her mate grasps her firmly and fertilzes the eggs as they leave her body. This process is known as amplexus.

Male Competition

Behaviorally, the males become more vocal and more aggressive, jostling with other males to find a vantage point to call from. Vocalizing takes place in an attempt to attract females for mating, and the chorus of calling males can be very loud in some species.

The call is of great importance for a large number of species. Experiments have shown that females are attracted to the loudest calls, and also those that last for longer periods, or are more complex. When suitable females become available, males will grasp them firmly with the forearms, and sometimes several males will attempt to mount the same female. This process, known as amplexus, will last for several hours, and the male will remain with the female until she has spawned.

Some species spawn communally over a very short, but synchronized, period. In this case, most of the males are able to find a mate. Spawning may only last for a few nights, and when completed, both males and females will disperse. In some species, however, the breeding season is rather more protracted, and the males will spend a good deal of time establishing territories and calling to attract the females, who visit a few at a time over a long period. In this case, it is more likely that a few dominant males will mate with a larger number of females, and many of the males will not get a chance to breed at all.

The dominant male in a colony is usually the one that starts calling first and continues for a longer period than all the others. His call will stimulate the others to start calling; their chorus may serve to confuse the females, giving others a chance to mate, or increase the volume and attract females from a wider area. Observations have shown that frogs that have a feeble call, and are therefore unlikely to attract a female for themselves, will sometimes lurk near a more powerful frog and try to get females attracted by his call. When the dominant male is occupied with one female, the interloper may be able to take advantage of another female.

Spawning

Spawning normally takes place in water, and only when a female has been grasped by a male. The eggs are released from the ovaries directly into the water through the cloaca, the common opening for the digestive, reproductive, and urinary systems. Moments after, the male releases the sperm and fertilization takes place in the water. The sperm must reach the eggs before the protective layer of jelly absorbs water and swells up. In order to achieve this, the male positions his cloaca as close to the female's as possible. This mating position, or amplexus, is maintained for several hours in some species, but once spawning is over and the pair separate, they have no further association, and, in most cases, take no further interest in their offspring.

The spawn itself shows a number of interesting variations. In all species there is an egg surrounded by protective jelly, but there are many adaptations to aid survival in different habitats. The egg, or ovum, contains the embryo, which will develop into a tadpole, and a supply of yolk, which is the food supply for the developing embryo. This part is visible as the black dot in the center of the clear jelly which surrounds it. On closer examination the black ovum is seen to be black above and gray below, the black color being derived from a layer of melanin, a black pigment which may offer some protection from ultra-violet radiation.

Eggs that are laid in shady conditions, such as under damp moss, lack melanin and have more yolk to sustain the developing embryo. Spawn is often deposited in the shallowest parts of ponds, providing the advantage of higher temperatures to speed development. The jelly offers protection from physical damage, from drying out, and from predators. In some species, it is impregnated with toxins

Mating can sometimes be a communal affair, and rival males may compete for a single female. These American toads, Bufo americana, *are locked in a battle for the right to mate with a female who has no say in which male eventually wins.*

The spawn masses of frogs and toads are easily identified, since toads always produce long strings of spawn, and frogs produce large masses or lay eggs individually. Each black dot in the protective jelly is a single embryo that will develop into a tadpole.

which potential predators, such as fish, find distasteful. In certain species, such as those that lay their eggs out of water, the jelly has a tough outer layer, or vitelline membrane, for added protection.

With species, such as the completely aquatic clawed toads, the eggs are laid singly, sometimes attaching themselves to stones and plants, or occasionally remaining floating just below the surface. For many frogs, the eggs are laid in one large clump; this is commonest in frogs that live in cooler climates where heat conservation may be important. A large mass of spawn will retain more heat than a scattering of single eggs. Many large masses of spawn will be even more efficient at retaining heat.

Most toads lay their eggs in long strings of jelly containing a double row of ova. The jelly swells up, and the eggs may spread to look like a single row. As they are releasing the eggs, the females move through pond weeds, entwining the spawn strings behind them. Very small species that lay their eggs in tiny pools of water, such as bromeliad vases, lay single eggs that float beneath the surface film. In this way, they have a good supply of oxygen for respiration.

A few species protect their eggs in a nest of foam. Mucus is whipped up into a foam with water, and the eggs are deposited inside it. They are protected in the nest from predators and also, from sudden changes in temperature or other weather conditions. The nest may be constructed in shallow water, deposited on damp ground, or stuck to a large leaf.

Some of the smallest species may only manage to lay a single egg at one spawning, but

the large toads may produce immense numbers of eggs at a time. The giant, or cane toad, *Bufo marinus* is thought to lay at least 30,000 eggs at a time, but the normal number for most of the medium-sized frogs and toads is a few hundred.

This great productivity is important, for tadpoles are an eagerly sought source of food for many creatures. Apart from being eaten by other amphibians, tadpoles are taken by fish, large aquatic insect larvae, birds, and small mammals. After their metamorphosis into small frogs, the slaughter continues, for there are just as many predators waiting for them on land. Of the many hundreds of embryos in the average mass of frog spawn, only one or two will ever achieve adulthood, causing the numbers in a given population to remain fairly constant from one year to the next.

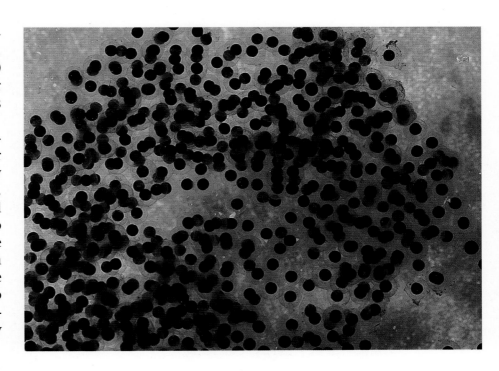

A newly laid egg mass floats in the water. Each egg is surrounded by a protective jelly which contains an embryo, which we see as a small black dot, and a yolk which will supply nourishment for the developing embryo.

Eggs are not always laid in water. Some species lay their tough–skinned eggs in clusters among leaf litter and usually remain to guard them until the tiny frogs emerge. The tadpole stage is by–passed in this way.

FOLLOWING PAGE: A pair of eastern spadefoot toads, male on the left, female on the right, stare each other down, showing the vertical pupils typical of the spadefoots. The external ear drum can be clearly seen on the side of the female's head.

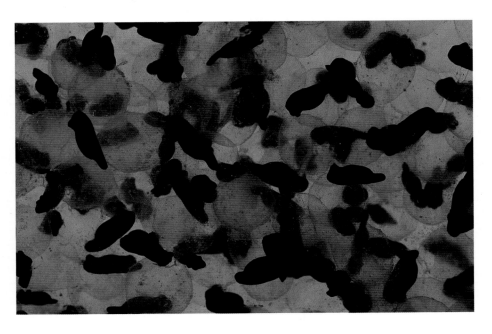

Once the embryo has developed to the point that a mouth is beginning to form, it emerges from the jelly and attaches itself to some stable surface in the water, such as pondweed. This period of development is known as the larval stage.

Tadpoles

Development of the embryo begins with the division of the ovum into two, then four, then eight cells, and so on, until countless numbers of small cells are formed. These envelop the yolk, and the developing embryo uses this for nourishment. The round ovum becomes kidney shaped, and then begins to form a recognizable

head and tail. The larva finds its way out of the jelly at a fairly early stage, before the limbs have developed, but just at the stage when the mouth is forming. It releases enzymes that break down the protective membranes and make them soft enough for it to break free. Once the tiny larva has wriggled out, it attaches itself to some pondweed and absorbs the rest of the yolk before starting to feed.

Tiny gills are visible soon after hatching, but these are soon covered by flaps of skin, each called an operculum, which grow over them from the sides of the head. The gills then remain enclosed in small chambers, and water circulates over them to aid respiration. They open to the outside through tiny holes called spiracles.

No limbs are visible at first, but as the tadpole feeds and grows, the hind limbs appear on either side of the tail. As the tail grows longer, the hind limbs also develop, growing longer, strongly resembling the limbs of adults. The front limbs appear eventually, in many species the left one pushing through the spiracle on the gill chamber. As the front limbs appear, the tail becomes shorter and the tadpole begins to resemble a miniature frog or toad. Its mouth gradually changes, and the

After only two days, these seven–day–old tadpoles show considerable development. The rate of growth varies from region to region and depends on the temperature. Tadpoles in arid locations develop rapidly, while those in colder climates may take two to three years to complete their metamorphosis.

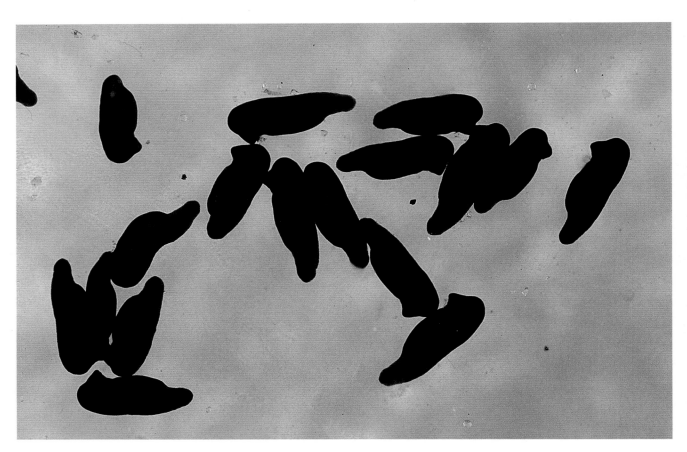

gills become less important for respiration as the tiny lungs develop. The froglet will spend more and more time out of water, until the tail has been completely absorbed. It will then move off into the type of habitat where it will spend most of its adult life.

The rate at which tadpoles complete their development varies greatly. For the majority of species living in temperate regions, tadpoles will develop from egg to frog in two to three months, if conditions are fairly stable, and they have an adequate food supply. Tadpoles of species living in very arid regions normally undergo a rapid metamorphosis; their breeding pools are likely to dry up very quickly, so they may be able to develop into froglets in about two weeks. The spadefoot toads and a number of species living in Africa and Australia can make use of temporary pools by having this rapid rate of development. The few species that live in cold regions or at high altitudes may take two or three years to metamorphose, overwintering as tadpoles.

Tadpoles often appear to be distributed randomly around a pond, but they may congregate around certain food sources. In some species the tadpoles form small shoals, keeping

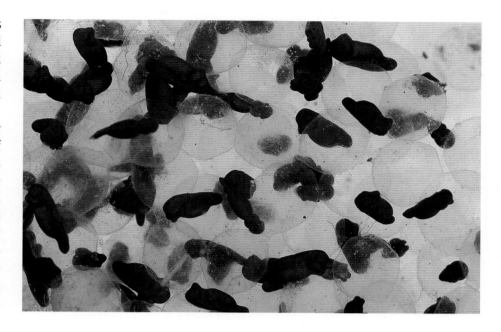

together and wriggling in formation around the pond. This may confuse predators, it may reduce any one individual's chances of being eaten, or it may help to stir up food. Some tadpoles are more solitary and nervous, diving for cover if disturbed, while those of some other species may be completely indifferent to disturbance of any form.

Soon after hatching, gills begin to develop on the larva. Then, the tail develops followed by the hind legs. Eventually the front limbs will appear. The tadpoles shown here are five days old.

Soon after hatching from the spawn mass, tadpoles develop their long tails to aid in swimming and sprout gills from the sides of the head. This is a time for feeding and growing, and tadpoles greedily devour a variety of foods. Many of them are eaten by fish before completing their development into tiny frogs.

Life Histories

In areas where there are relatively few species of frogs, they tend to spawn in open water, but where many species occur, they will exploit a variety of habitats. In parts of Europe and North America, where there are only a handful of species, some will breed in open water, but near the margins of pools, while others, especially toads, will breed in deeper, weedy places where they can entwine their spawn strings around plant stems. Others will choose the margins of a pool where the water is shallowest and also the warmest.

One area of the Amazonian rain forest in Ecuador is known to have eighty-one species of frogs and toads living in an area of 2,500–5,000 acres (1–2 hectares). With so many species living in such close proximity, avoiding competition is very important. Some achieve this by breeding in the same habitats but at different seasons. Others have exploited a great range of niches from open water in rivers and pools, to the tiniest pools of water in bromeliad flowers. Some have dispensed with water altogether and lay their eggs on land, while others carry their larvae around with them.

Aquatic development.

About half of the world's frog and toad species breed in open water, laying their eggs in clumps, in strings randomly in the water, floating in rafts, or by attaching them to aquatic plants. There may a synchronized mass spawning of all of the frogs in a given population, or several intermittent spawnings during a long breeding season. The advantage of large bodies of water is that they are unlikely to dry out during the time needed to complete metamorphosis; also, they will have plenty of food. However, there is also the likelihood that competition will be severe, and there is always the risk of predators being present.

As the fore limbs, head, and mouth of the tadpole start to develop, the tail begins to diminish in prominence, Already this pinewoods tree-frog tadpole is beginning to take on the characteristics of an adult frog.

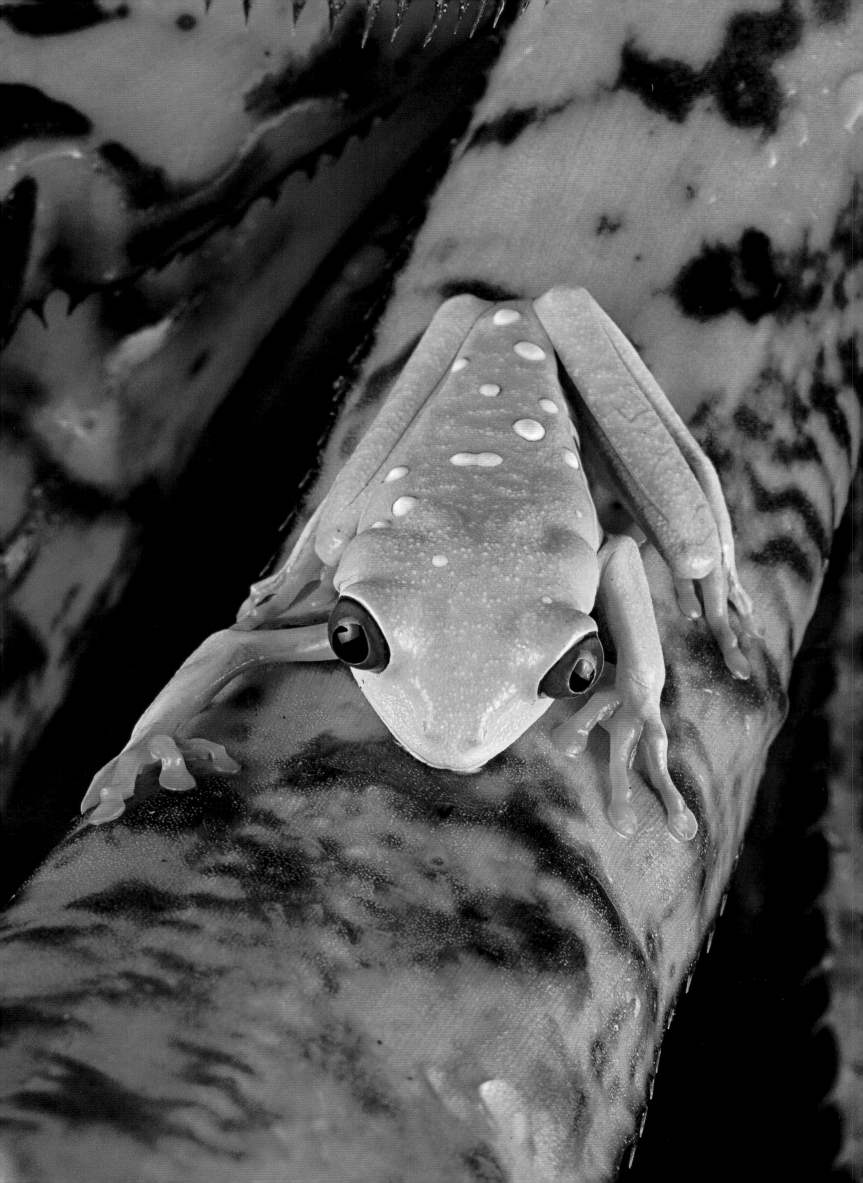

A few species use small temporary pools for breeding. These pools may be small puddles, animal hoof prints, wheel ruts, or tree hollows. In tropical regions where rainfall is frequent, they are unlikely to dry out. Such places may not contain much food, so the larvae will need a good yolk supply in the egg to sustain them. In addition, they are normally free from predators so development can continue unhindered. Oxygen supplies are often low in temporary pools, so the larvae are normally active near the surface of the pool where oxygen exchange with the air takes place.

Fast flowing streams are difficult habitats for tadpoles to develop in, as the spawn and small larvae are likely to be swept away. In order to overcome this, the eggs are usually attached to stones or deposited in backwaters or plunge pools. The tadpoles normally have a streamlined shape and often have sucker-like mouths to aid adhesion to rocks. In streams with gravelly beds, some tadpoles live in the spaces between the stones, feeding on tiny particles swept down by the current. Fast flowing water has the advantage of being highly oxygenated and is normally free from pollution.

Unusual Breeding Sites

Tree frogs are among the species that have exploited the water that collects in tree hollows and in bromeliad flowers. The central part of the bromeliad flower, a common epiphytic plant of tropical forests in Central and South America, forms a structure known as a vase, and this will contain sufficient water for a few tadpoles to develop in. These species spend the whole of their lives up in the trees, not needing to come down to the ground at all for either food or breeding sites. Bromeliads do not occur in Africa or Asia, but tree ferns, palms, and other lush tropical forest species have leaf formations that sometimes allow small pools of water to form; these have been exploited by the Old World species equivalent to the South American tree frogs.

Horned frogs, like this large species, Ceratophrys cranwelli, *from South America, are forest–floor dwellers, using shallow pools for breeding, but spending most of their lives concealed in damp leaf litter.*

The tiny maroon–eyed tree frog, Agalychnis callidryas, *from the rain forests of Central America has the perfect coloration to help it merge with its surroundings in dense foliage. Only its eyes, important features in courtship displays, break up the leaf–green body color. When it keeps still it is very difficult for predators to spot.*

The adult Costa Rican arrow–poison (or dart–poison) frog, Dendrobates pumilio, *brightly marked as a warning, carries its tadpole on its back, on the way to deposit it in water trapped in the leaves of a bromeliad plant.*

A few species, such as some of the larger tree frogs of South America, construct small pools on the ground near to streams, and these fill with water by seepage through the soil. Males construct these nests, and then call to the females from them. They aggressively eject any males who might approach, but encourage females to lay eggs in the shallow water in their pool nests. This may occur over several nights, causing these pools often to contain eggs and tadpoles at varying stages of development, derived from several different females. A rise in water level of the main river nearby will sometimes inundate the tiny pool and disperse the tadpoles over a wider area.

In order to avoid predation, some species lay their eggs, not in the water, but attached to overhanging leaves. When the tadpoles hatch, they drop from the jelly into the water.

Sometimes the leaves are folded over and glued together to form a tube to further protect the eggs. The glass frogs of South America and the leaf folding frogs of Africa use emergent vegetation such as reeds, and overhanging marginal plants. Sometimes one of the parents will stay with the eggs and wait until the tadpoles emerge. They may need a little help to slide down the leaf into the water, and the parent will be on hand to do this.

Terrestrial Spawning

Some terrestrial breeders lay their eggs on land that is near water and prone to flooding, such as damp grassland on the margins of a shallow lake or river. The males usually stay on guard until the eggs are swept away. Development takes place very slowly at first, and only begins properly when the eggs are in water.

Other terrestrial spawners, that lay their eggs near water, do not depend upon flooding. Their tadpoles hatch on land, and then wriggle through damp grass or loose soil to reach the water. Other species will actually show some parental care and carry their larvae to a suitable body of water. This is usually done by the males who attach the tadpoles to their backs with a mucus secretion; this keeps them in place until they get to the water and submerge. The mucus is soluble in water and so breaks up and releases the tadpoles when they have reached safety.

Exceptions to the Rule

Unlike most frogs and toads that spawn in water or on land, a few species carry their eggs with them at all times until they hatch, and then the tadpoles are released. The best known example of this is the aptly named midwife toad. In this species, the male carries strings of eggs on his back until the tadpoles hatch. Other variations on this theme occur when the eggs are carried by females, or in the case of the "marsupial" frogs where the eggs develop inside special pouches.

The female of a very rare Australian frog species carries the eggs inside her stomach until the tadpoles develop completely; when they reach this stage, they are disgorged. A few species lay large eggs in which development takes place from ovum to fully metamorphosed frog without a free-living tadpole stage.

The female Surinam toad carries about one hundred eggs in individual chambers on her back, where they develop fully into tiny toads before leaving the chambers to swim away. For

The African reed frogs, Hyperolius, *are common and widespread species in southern and eastern Africa, inhabiting swamps and marshes where there is sufficient emergent vegetation to hide them. They breed in winter, making use of temporary pools for spawning.*

a short period prior to leaving, their limbs protrude from these chambers, giving the female a very odd appearance. Once the young have left their protective cells, the female sheds her skin and resumes a more normal appearance.

The most advanced stage in the development of the eggs has been reached in those species that have internal fertilization and retain the eggs inside the oviducts, while they complete their development. The female then gives birth to fully formed young frogs.

Parental care

Most species take no care of their offspring beyond laying the eggs in a suitable environment. Some of the larger species lay very large numbers of eggs to ensure that at least some will survive the effects of disease or predation.

However, an exception to this is the small group of species that lay their eggs in bromeliad flower "vases." These tiny pools of water, high in the forest canopy, cannot provide enough food for developing tadpoles, so the female frogs visit them every few days to deposit a large yolk-rich food egg in the flower for the tadpoles to feed on.

It is normally the small species that show a greater degree of parental care. Since they can only lay a few eggs, they take greater care of them, sometimes simply by remaining nearby to guard them, or in a few cases, by moving the tadpoles to safer places, or by providing food.

The oak toad, Bufo quercicus, *is a very small species, found, despite its name, in pine woods in the southern United States. What it lacks in size, it makes up for in attractive and very varied markings. It is often abundant, and its high–pitched peeping calls can be heard on rainy evenings. Oak toads rarely exceed 1.3 inches (3.3 cm) in length.*

The Cape Rain frog, Breviceps gibbosus, *from the Cape peninsula of South Africa, has a small head and mouth and a greatly inflated body. Its markings and warty skin are ideal for camouflage on a forest floor. Its eggs are laid in underground chambers.*

THE WORLD OF FROGS AND TOADS

A common misconception about frogs and toads is that they spend all of their lives in water. A few species are entirely aquatic, only coming to the surface of the water to breathe, but many more are entirely terrestrial, living on the ground, or underground, in trees, or even in deserts. It is true that for most species water in some form or other is essential for breeding. The majority of species inhabit areas of relatively high humidity and high temperatures and live in close proximity to water.

Aquatic Species

Very few species are found in large bodies of water, such as deep lakes, because so few species are entirely aquatic. The African clawed toads, *Xenopus*, and some frogs from lakes high in the Andes in South America are exceptions to this. Aquatic species normally have well developed webbed hind feet and nostrils positioned on the tops of their heads. Their colors are usually rather dull to aid camouflage; this is very important to aquatic species, as there are many potentially dangerous predators in deep water.

Swamps and marshes are important habitats for frogs, as humidity is normally high here. Water for breeding is rarely in short supply, and there is usually plenty of food available. Ponds are highly favored, as they are often warmer than larger water bodies and will have fewer predators, especially fish, living in them.

Running water has been exploited by some species, as there are several distinct advantages over swamps. Oxygen levels are high in cool, flowing water, and there is normally a regular supply of food available. Humidity is also high near streams and rivers.

The large Argentine horned frog, Ceratophrys ornata, has striking markings, but these help it blend in with its surroundings in densely vegetated swamps and marshes, and on the forest floor. This excellent camouflage protects it from predators and helps conceal it from its prey.

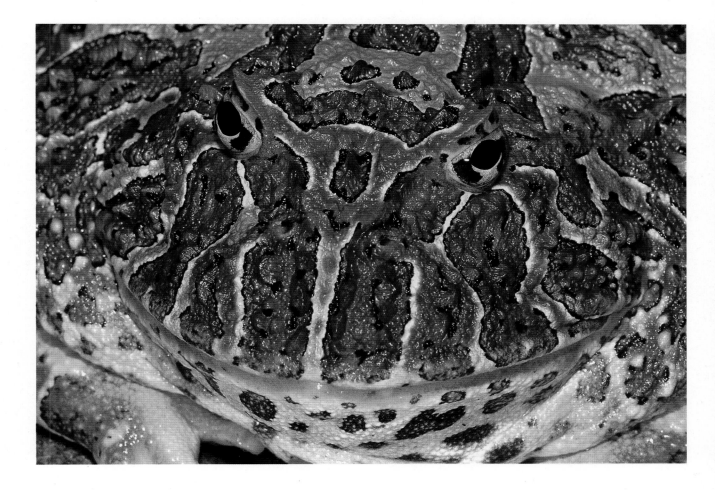

This bullfrog from Florida shows typical colors for a marsh dwelling frog. Living among duckweeds and water plants, green is the best color to be, and similar species in other parts of the world show the same adaptations to life in an aquatic environment. Reaching a length of up to 6 inches (15 cm), this is the largest frog in North America.

Typical of the other "green frogs," the southern leopard frog, Rana sphenocephala, has markings suitable for camouflage in swamps and marshes; in summer it may move away from the water and live in damp grassland. It is an excellent jumper and swimmer and very common in the southern United States.

The bronze frog, Rana clamitans clamitans, widespread in swamps and beside streams in the southeastern United States, is a secretive species, spending much time sheltering under logs and in shady hollows. The call of the male is a quite distinctive single staccato note.

FOLLOWING PAGE:
*The smallest frog
in North America
is the little grass
frog,* Limnaoedes
ocularis, *found in
the southeastern
United States in
grassy areas on
the edges of ponds
and swamps. It
rarely exceeds
5/8 inch (1.6 cm)
in length. Its fee-
ble call is so high
pitched and
insect–like that
some people are
unable to hear it.
It is able to climb
in tall grasses,
but rarely into
trees or shrubs.*

*Long legs give
the red–eyed tree
frog great agility
and make it easy to
climb through
vegetation; hop-
ping would not
be a very good
form of locomotion
here, so limbs
and feet are adapt-
ed for climbing.*

Forest Dwellers

Many species live in forests, although most of these are found in tropical forests where most of the available micro-habitats, from the upper canopy to the forest floor, have been exploit- ed. The forest-dwelling species show good adaptations to an arboreal existence by being able to climb through the trees, jump easily from branch to branch, and even glide through the forest on outstretched limbs. Forest–floor species are usually cryptically camouflaged and have tough skins and projec- tions from the body to deter predators. The frogs that live in the trees have brighter mark- ings and are sometimes green, so that they blend with the vegetation.

The river frog, Rana hecksheri, *widespread in the southeastern United States, is a large, predominantly gray–brown species which has distinctive light spots on the lips. Adults are fairly confident and easily observed, and are best detected by the deep, snore–like call heard from riverside vegetation.*

The confusingly named green frog, Rana clamitans melanota, *of the southern United States may have more brown on its body than green, but there is always green coloration around the mouth. This is an abundant species wherever there is shallow fresh water, ranging from streams and marshes to the edges of large lakes.*

The Javan flying frog, Rhacophorus reinwardtii, *shows one of the more remarkable adaptations to life in the tree canopy, having the ability to glide through the canopy on outstretched limbs and extended digits supporting a thin skin. This enables it to exploit larger areas of the forest than other tree–dwelling frogs, and escape rapidly from predators.*

Extreme Habitats

Deserts would seem to be the most unlikely habitats in which to find amphibians, but a few species have adapted to this inhospitable environment by burrowing and remaining hidden during very dry periods, only emerging in periods of rainfall for a brief period of feeding and breeding. For most of their lives, species like spadefoot toads live in underground chambers, which they have excavated and lined with layers of mucus and shed skin.

Frogs and Toads as Travelers

Frogs and toads are mobile creatures, but most species do not stray very far from their home ranges. Though they are sedentary for much of their lives, remaining in hiding to escape predation or desiccation, they often move around

Deserts appear to be the most unlikely places to find frogs. Nevertheless, several species, including this African bullfrog in Kalahari-Gemsbok National Park, manage to survive long dry spells in underground chambers. When the rainy season starts, they emerge to breed.

An eastern spadefoot toad, Scaphiopus holbrooki, *so named because of the single sharp–edged, black spade on each hind foot, shelters beneath a toadstool during a rainstorm. In this weather, food is easy to find, since slugs and other forest–floor invertebrates also emerge to feed.*

The hour–glass tree frog, Hyla ebreccata, *from Central America, relies on its natural colors to blend in with plant stems and fruits. Its habit of remaining motionless for long periods protects it from predators like snakes and birds.*

at night in search of food. There seems to be little interchange between different populations of the same species if they are isolated from each other by even a short distance.

Some frogs undertake quite dramatic journeys, however, but this is normally by accident rather than design. Tiny tree frogs have been known to travel half way around the world in crates of bananas and other tropical fruits, while tadpoles have found their way into aquariums by being carried in pond weed collected for the tropical fish trade. One of the most dramatic ways for frogs and toads to move around is to be picked up in a tornado. Stories of frogs raining from the sky have some foundation in fact, as occasionally water can be sucked up from swamps by a tornado, and if there are tiny frogs in it, they will be carried along and dropped a great distance away.

Life Span

Most frogs and toads do not die of old age. They are prey species in their habitats, taken by a wide range of larger creatures, so their potential longevity in a predator-free, wild

environment is not known. Some of the tiny tree and glass frogs have very short lives, maturing quickly, breeding once or twice, and only surviving for a year or two. Some of the commoner large frogs, such as the European common frog, take up to three years to reach maturity before they can breed, and if they escape predation, they may live for several more years.

Recording life spans of frogs living in the wild is very difficult, but for those in captivity it is far easier. However, this can not be taken as a reliable guide to how long it is possible for them to live in nature, since in captivity they are provided with food at regular intervals, they are safe from predators, and are kept in a carefully managed environment free from the risk of natural disasters such as droughts or freezing conditions. In these highly favorable circumstances, many species can live to a great age. There are reports of a European common toad living for over fifty years, and the author's own pet African clawed toad is thirty years old at the time of writing and is showing no signs of aging.

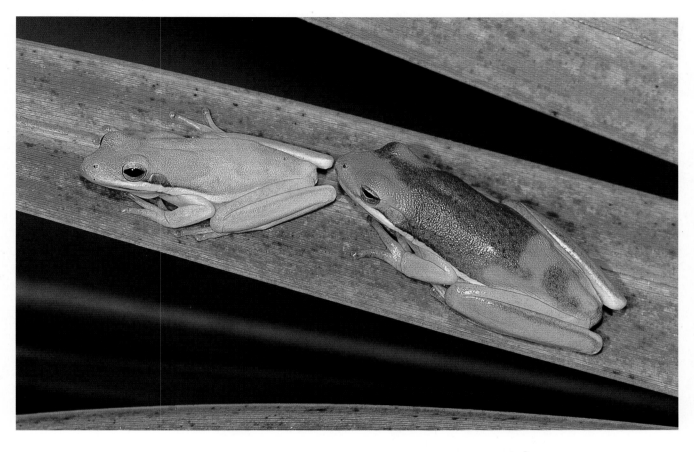

Most frogs have a symmetrical pattern of markings, but these green tree frogs, Hyla cinerea, from Florida, show an unusual pattern that matches the random growths of lichens on palm fronds where they usually rest.

There seems to be no limit to the variations in size, shape, colors, and habits of frogs and toads. One of the most unusual is this minute glass frog from Costa Rica. It is one of the smallest of all amphibians, and here, it sits neatly inside a cup fungus, growing out of a rotten tree trunk.

The small size of tree frogs, such as this cross–banded tree frog, Smilisca puma, from Nicaragua, enable them to exploit habitats not available to their larger, ground and swamp dwelling relatives. They are safer here, as most predators can not reach them, and have adapted well to life in vegetation.

Threats to Survival

The greatest danger facing frogs and toads is the destruction of their habitats. Vast areas of tropical forest are destroyed every year; these are the richest habitats for frogs and toads, and many species are now very scarce and even on the verge of extinction as a result of the loss of important areas of forest.

Pollution of waterways is a serious threat to a number of species who spend much of their time in or near water. The use of pesticides by farmers and gardeners has reduced the availability of food to frog species, especially those that live in relatively close proximity to humans. Introduction of alien predators in some habitats has made inroads into small and specialized populations of endangered species. Predatory fish and mammals like mink have had a devastating effect on some species.

The need to live in two habitats, land and water, means that if one is destroyed, the frog is unable to complete its life-cycle, so increasing urbanization, intensive agriculture, road building, and mineral exploitation have all reduced the amount of undisturbed habitat left for frogs and toads to live in.

Those that have tried to live alongside humans in urban and agricultural areas have to contend with introduced predators such as cats and dogs. Large numbers are squashed on roads as they migrate towards breeding ponds, and many suffer by becoming trapped in drainage systems.

Exploitation for food is also endangering a few species which happen to live near human

The masked puddle frog, Smilisca, from Costa Rica, is preyed on by bats. In order to confuse their predators, groups of these tiny frogs synchronize their calls at night.

Suction–pad toes help this Cuban tree frog, Hyla septentrionalis, climb and maneuver its way in and out of hiding places. Predatory birds and snakes pursue the frogs in the trees, so secure hiding places are very important to them.

The aptly–named shovel–nosed frogs, Triprion spatulatus, from Mexico, have very distinctive ridged heads to aid in burrowing in soft ground.

The Amazonian lichen frog, Hyla marmorata, *shows a remarkable adaptation to life in the rain forest, closely resembling the irregular colonies of lichens and lower plants that colonize the surfaces of leaves in the rain forest. Its flattened shape and ability to remain motionless for long periods make it very difficult to find.*

A pair of painted–belly monkey Frogs, Phyllomedusa sauvagei, show off their white–spotted undersides while resting on a bromeliad in an Argentine forest. This species is able to protect itself from dry conditions by wiping a waxy secretion over its body.

settlements. One species, the edible frog, is regularly consumed in Europe, and its numbers have now declined to such an extent, partly through exploitation and partly through habitat loss, that other local species are now being taken instead. In addition, alien species from other parts of the world are imported to make up the deficit. In parts of Asia, several large species are collected in huge numbers for local consumption or for export.

The Importance of Conservation

Frogs and toads are highly beneficial creatures in many places where they share a habitat with humans. They consume huge quantities of potentially harmful insects and other invertebrates, such as slugs, which can be damaging to crops. Farmers and gardeners should do all they can to encourage frogs and toads, as they will become very efficient pest controllers.

Frogs and toads are an important link in the food chain in many ecosystems, providing sustenance for larger predators such as birds or snakes. Their great productivity of eggs provides a surplus of tadpoles and tiny froglets that are the principal source of food for many other vertebrates.

Individuals can help frogs and toads in various ways. Constructing a garden pond is likely to encourage frogs and toads to move in and take up residence in many parts of the world. As long as the pond has no large fish in it, frogs will be able to breed successfully and become useful additions to the garden, feeding on invertebrates which might otherwise trouble the gardener. Gardeners who know that they have resident frogs and toads should take great care with the use of pesticides, avoiding them completely, if at all possible. Providing a few hiding places such as log piles or upturned flower pots helps them keep safe from predators, and keeping the pond free of fish ensures the survival of their offspring.

The Asian leaf toad, Megophrys nasuta, *does its best to blend in with the leaf litter on the forest floor and shows one of the most remarkable forms of camouflage of any amphibian. Unless it moves, it is almost completely invisible to passersby.*

In the public area, concerned citizens can let their voices be heard by supporting sound environmental and development policies and legislation. Letters to local and national officials do have an effect, especially if significant numbers are received. People can also support any of the many environmental groups and study centers that promote conservation and strive to make the public more aware of the problems faced by many species today. Even a modest contribution to these efforts can make a difference.

Frogs and toads have been around for many millions of years and live in their environment without harming it; it is now our responsibility to safeguard their future.

Barking tree frogs exploit a wide range of habitats from swampy pools to dry loose soils and many types of trees and leafy shrubs. Its bright green colors may vary, and it usually shows a high degree of spotting when the green fades to yellow or gray.

Many insects settle on the lichen–covered bark of trees, and some tree frogs have exploited this habitat. This Ecuadorian tree frog, Hyla, is perfectly matched to the mottled gray lichens, and with its eyes closed it will not be spotted by any predators.

INDEX

*Page numbers in **bold-face** type indicate photo captions.*